SUPER
SANDCASTLE·
Going Green

WHAT
IN THE
WORLD
IS A
GREEN HOME?

Oona Gaarder-Juntti

Consulting Editor, Diane Craig, M.A./Reading Specialist

ABDO
Publishing Company

Published by ABDO Publishing Company, 8000 West 78th Street, Edina, Minnesota 55439. Copyright © 2011 by Abdo Consulting Group, Inc. International copyrights reserved in all countries. No part of this book may be reproduced in any form without written permission from the publisher. Super SandCastle™ is a trademark and logo of ABDO Publishing Company.

Printed in the United States of America, North Mankato, Minnesota
052010
092010

Editor: Katherine Hengel
Content Developer: Nancy Tuminelly
Cover and Interior Design and Production: Oona Gaarder-Juntti, Mighty Media
Photo Credits: AbleStock, iStockphoto (Allsee, Carlsson Inc. Photography, Sebastien Cote), Shutterstock

Library of Congress Cataloging-in-Publication Data

Gaarder-Juntti, Oona, 1979-
  What in the world is a green home? / Oona Gaarder-Juntti.
    p. cm. -- (Going green)
  ISBN 978-1-61613-189-0
  1. Ecological houses--Juvenile literature. I. Title.
  TH4860.G33 2011
  640--dc22
                        9509   2010004340

Super SandCastle™ books are created by a team of professional educators, reading specialists, and content developers around five essential components— phonemic awareness, phonics, vocabulary, text comprehension, and fluency— to assist young readers as they develop reading skills and strategies and increase their general knowledge. All books are written, reviewed, and leveled for guided reading, early reading intervention, and Accelerated Reader® programs for use in shared, guided, and independent reading and writing activities to support a balanced approach to literacy instruction.

ABOUT SUPER SANDCASTLE™

Bigger Books for Emerging Readers

Grades K–4

Created for library, classroom, and at-home use, Super SandCastle™ books support and engage young readers as they develop and build literacy skills and will increase their general knowledge about the world around them. Super SandCastle™ books are an extension of SandCastle™, the leading preK–3 imprint for emerging and beginning readers. Super SandCastle™ features a larger trim size for more reading fun.

Let Us Know

Super SandCastle™ would like to hear your stories about reading this book. What was your favorite page? Was there something hard that you needed help with? Share the ups and downs of learning to read. We want to hear from you! Send us an e-mail.

sandcastle@abdopublishing.com

Contact us for a complete list of SandCastle™, Super SandCastle™, and other nonfiction and fiction titles from ABDO Publishing Company.

www.abdopublishing.com • 8000 West 78th Street Edina, MN 55439 • 800-800-1312 • 952-831-1632 fax

Contents

WHAT IN THE WORLD IS BEING GREEN?

Being green means taking care of the earth. Many things on our planet are connected. When one thing changes, it can cause something else to change. That's why the way we treat the earth is so important. Keeping the earth healthy can seem like a big job. You can help by saving energy and **resources** every day.

Saving Energy

Our homes need energy. We often burn oil and coal to make energy. When we do, we create greenhouse gases. These gases go into the air. They can trap the sun's heat and make the earth warmer. This is called **global** warming. Saving energy reduces greenhouse gases.

Protecting Resources

Soil, trees, water, and air are natural **resources**. Sometimes we waste or harm the earth's resources. For example, we waste water when we leave the faucet running.

GREEN HOMES

We use a lot of energy in our homes. Energy keeps the temperature in our homes comfortable. We use energy to cook food and keep it fresh. Computers and TVs use energy too. We can save **resources** by saving energy. There are a lot of things we can do!

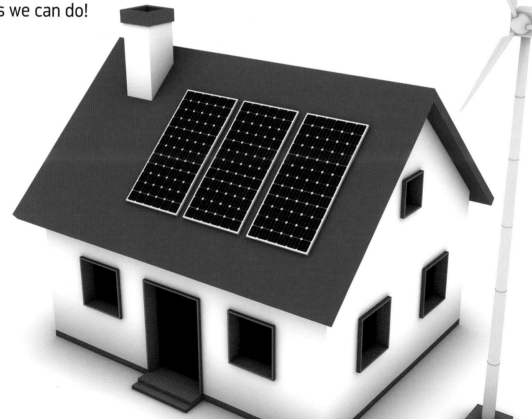

Did you know?

Most of the energy used in homes is for heating and cooling.

Did you know?

Recycling one **aluminum** can saves enough energy to run a TV for 3 hours.

Did you know?

Every minute in the shower uses 4 to 6 gallons (15 to 23 L) of water.

IN A GREEN WORLD

What we do around our homes affects the earth. Here are some ways to go green!

Trees provide natural shade.

The best way to recycle food scraps is to put them in a **compost** bin!

Grow your own food in your backyard! Fresh food tastes better and is good for you.

IN A GREEN WORLD

Homes use a lot of energy! Here are some ways that you can save energy at home.

Open the **drapes** and use sunlight when you can.

Plug electronics into a power strip instead of the wall. Switch the power strip off when you are done.

IN A GREEN WORLD

Go green in your room! Here are some simple things you can do to help the earth.

Turn TVs, computers, and stereos off when you're not using them.

Use compact **fluorescent** lightbulbs (CFLs).

HOW YOU CAN HELP

Everyone knows the 3 Rs. Reduce, Reuse, and Recycle. Do you know how to practice the 3 Rs at home? The next few pages will show you how! Think about what you use, how you use it, and where it goes when you're done with it. Try to make things last. Reuse things whenever you can. There are many simple things that you can do!

Energy Detective

Make a map of your house. Mark all of your windows and doors on the map. Hold a ribbon near the edge of each window and door. If the ribbon moves, you've found a **draft**. Mark it on your map. Then tell an adult. Weather stripping can stop drafts and save energy.

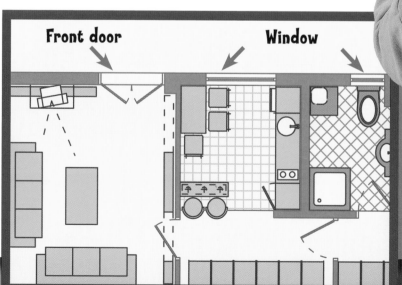

Front door   Window

Use it Wisely!

The water that comes out of your faucet is special. It has been cleaned and **filtered**. It took energy to do that! When you waste tap water, you're wasting energy.

Here are some ways to save tap water.

- Take short showers instead of baths.
- Keep a pitcher of water in the refrigerator. Don't let the tap water run until it is cold!
- Turn off the water when you brush your teeth.
- Check your house for leaky faucets.

Swap with Friends!

Do you have old clothes, toys, or books at home? Your friends probably do too. You could trade! Ask your parents for permission first. Then invite your friends over. Tell them to bring their old things over for a swap!

Donating your old things is a great idea too. If you aren't using something, give it to someone who will! When we find ways to reuse things, we're helping the earth!

Check out books, CDs, and DVDs from your library. It's a very green way to enjoy new things!

Second Life

Find a good spot for recycling bins at your house. Make labels for each bin. **Aluminum** cans, cardboard, glass, newspapers, and plastic bottles can be recycled. They can be made into new products! Making things from recycled materials uses less energy and **resources**.

Are there things in your garbage that you could reuse? Newspapers and paper bags can be wrapping paper. Jars and containers can be reused to store things. Or they can be pencil holders! Be creative! See how many things you can reuse.

Aluminum is an amazing material. It can be recycled over and over again. On the surface of the earth, there is a lot of aluminum. There is more aluminum in the earth's surface than any other metal.

Change a Bulb

When lightbulbs burn out, replace them with compact **fluorescent** lightbulbs (CFLs). CFLs use less energy than other lightbulbs. They provide the same amount of light! They also last ten times longer than regular bulbs.

Replace one lightbulb in your house with a CFL. You'll save enough energy to light 3 million homes for a year!

Switch it Off!

When electronic **devices** are plugged in, they use energy. Even if they are turned off! Try using power strips. Plug several electronics into one strip. Then you can easily turn the power strip on and off to save energy.

Remember to turn off all lights and appliances when you leave the room.

Tell your parents about using power strips. You can save energy and money!

LET'S THINK GREEN

There is a lot to learn about green homes! Remember that small things count. That is why it is important to build green habits now! What other things can you do to make a difference?

Taking care of the earth is everyone's responsibility. That means kids and adults! Talk with your family and friends about being green at home. Let's all work hard together and think green!

TAKE THE GREEN PLEDGE

I promise to help the earth every day by doing things in a different way.

At home I can help by:

- ♻ Turning off the water when brushing my teeth.
- ♻ Donating items I'm not using to someone who will.
- ♻ Helping my family recycle.
- ♻ Plugging things into a power strip instead of the wall.

GLOSSARY

aluminum – a light metal often used to make cans and bottles.

compost – a mixture of natural materials, such as food scraps and lawn clippings, that can turn into fertilizer over time.

device – a piece of equipment that has a certain job.

draft – a stream of cold air.

drape – heavy cloth hung in front of a window.

filter – to clean a liquid by passing it through a device that removes any matter floating in it.

fluorescent – giving out a bright light, such as ultraviolet light.

global – having to do with the whole earth.

resource – the supply or source of something. A *natural resource* is a resource found in nature such as water or trees.

solar panel – a device that turns the sun's light into energy.